D1399534

Soapylove

BY DEBBIE CHIALTAS

North Light Books
Cincinnati, Ohio
www.mycraftivity.com

13 12 11 10 09 5 4 3 2 1

Distributed in Canada by Fraser Direct
100 Armstrong Avenue
Georgetown, ON, Canada L7G 5S4
Tel: (905) 877-4411

Distributed in the U.K. and Europe by David & Charles
Brunel House, Newton Abbot, Devon, TQ12 4PU, England
Tel: (+44) 1626 323200, Fax: (+44) 1626 323319
E-mail: postmaster@davidandcharles.co.uk

Distributed in Australia by Capricorn Link
P.O. Box 704, S. Windsor, NSW 2756 Australia
Tel: (02) 4577-3555

Library of Congress Cataloging-in-Publication Data
Chialtas, Debbie.
   Soapylove / by Debbie Chialtas. -- 1st ed.
      p. cm.
   Includes bibliographical references and index.
   ISBN 978-1-60061-170-4 (pbk. : alk. paper)
   1. Soap. I. Title.
   TP991.C426 2009
   668'.12--dc22
                                    2009006462

media
an imprint of F+W Media, Inc.
www.fwmedia.com

metric conversion chart

to convert	to	multiply by
Inches	Centimeters	2.54
Centimeters	Inches	0.4
Feet	Centimeters	30.5
Centimeters	Feet	0.03
Yards	Meters	0.9
Meters	Yards	1.1
Sq. Inches	Sq. Centimeters	6.45
Sq. Centimeters	Sq. Inches	0.16
Sq. Feet	Sq. Meters	0.09
Sq. Meters	Sq. Feet	10.8
Sq. Yards	Sq. Meters	0.8
Sq. Meters	Sq. Yards	1.2
Pounds	Kilograms	0.45
Kilograms	Pounds	2.2
Ounces	Grams	28.3
Grams	Ounces	0.035

EDITOR: JULIE HOLLYDAY
DESIGNER: KELLY O'DELL
PRODUCTION COORDINATOR: GREG NOCK
PHOTOGRAPHER: RIC DELIANTONI
      AND CHRISTINE POLOMSKY
PHOTO STYLIST: LAUREN EMMERLING

dedication

This book is dedicated to my incredibly loving and supportive husband, Jim, who quietly tolerates my obsessive soap making; my kids, who inspired my leap from corporate slave to WAHM (Work at Home Mom); SoapyErin, who is both an amazing professional and friend; Jennifer Perkins, who recommended me as an author for this book; and my online pals who cheer me on through every soapy drama and milestone!

Thank you also to the Lavigna and Chialtas families, who are always ready and eager to help me, no matter what the request. You're the best!

about the author

Debbie Chialtas is a self-taught melt and pour soap crafter with a bachelor's degree in fine art from the Academy of Art University in San Francisco. Her background is in fashion design, which plays a big role in her soap inspiration. She has been an Etsy featured artist, appeared as a guest on DIY *Craft Lab* and has taught soap crafting at Otion's Soap Making Weekend Intensive. Her Web site, www.soapylove.com, is where she sells her signature item—Soapsicles—as well as tutorials and post any workshops she may be teaching.

She currently lives in San Diego with her husband, Jim, and their two adorable kids.

table of contents

☆ using molds creatively 48

☆ color techniques 74

☆ unusual tools & materials 100

introduction

Welcome to the world of Soapylove!
Prepare to be inspired. Bright colors, delicious
themes and lots of fun tips have been brought together
to help you make the most amazing soaps you have ever
laid your eyes on!

Melt and pour soap crafting has never been so innovative or
stylish—and the best thing is that it's easy to do! With clear steps
and lots of great pictures, you will amaze yourself and have a great
time doing it. For parties, gifts or just to dazzle your bathroom, these
soaps will bring oohs and aahs.

My favorite part of soap crafting is creating something completely
beautiful and totally useful at the same time! As you flip through
this book deciding which to make first, you will see that there is a
big variety of looks to choose from. Donuts, UFOs,
silhouettes and checkers are all found here.
What they have in common is a love of
color, a sense of humor and, most of
all, tons of style.

So come on in and start creating.
You're bound to "Feel the Love!"

materials & techniques

If you have never tried melt and pour soap crafting before, you're in luck! The materials are easy to find and the steps are not complicated.

Most of the supplies will be in your local craft shop and you may already have many of them in your kitchen. What you can't find locally will be easily found online. Each tutorial in this book has the materials listed in the beginning, but this section will tell you more about the major supplies and what they do.

MELT & POUR (AKA "GLYCERIN") SOAP BASE

This is a premade soap that comes in clear or white blocks. The white is the same as the clear base, but with a white colorant. It's a basic soap you can melt in the microwave, add colorants and fragrance to, and remold in any flexible container you have. Please note that you can't do this with any bar soap you buy in the grocery store. You need to specifically buy "melt and pour" soap made for crafting.

It's often called glycerin soap base because extra glycerin has been added (along with some other ingredients) to make it clear and remeltable. Many people misinterpret this name thinking it's only made of glycerin, and that's not correct. The brand you buy may have the ingredients listed on the package.

Clear soap base doesn't look the same from all companies. For some projects, I have specified "Ultra Clear" to make sure the soap does not have a yellow tint to it. Any company's white soap base will be fine, though.

To melt the soap base, follow the super simple instructions on page 9.

Soap crafting is extremely easy to clean up. The base is nontoxic, so any cup or spoon you use can be washed and used in your kitchen for food again. But don't make a common mistake—always prewash your supplies before putting them in your dishwasher or you might have a Brady moment (mountains of bubbles all over your kitchen)! See page 9 for easy clean-up instructions.

RUBBING ALCOHOL

This is your best friend, and you will need it for every project. Just fill a small spray bottle with isopropyl rubbing alcohol from a drugstore and you're ready to go.

Rubbing alcohol does a few things:

☆ A few light sprays will pop any surface bubbles when you're done pouring the soap. We wouldn't want any imperfections on these beautiful soaps, now would we?

☆ It makes soap layers adhere to each other. If you pour a layer of soap, let it set, then pour another layer of soap without spraying the set soap with alcohol first, the soap will split into two layers and ruin your day. Don't worry, I'll tell you when to spray in each project, so have your bottle handy. See page 17 for some general instructions and tips for adding layers to a project.

☆ You can dilute powdered colorants with it before adding to your soap. If you add powders directly to your melted soap base, you'll get lumps. To avoid this, dissolve the powder in a few squirts of alcohol in a small cup, and then add it to the soap base. Follow the instructions on pages 11 and 13 for beautiful color additions.

TECHNIQUE:
CUTTING & MELTING SOAP BASE

Cut soap base
Using a kitchen knife and a cutting board, cut the desired amount of soap base into approximately ½" (1cm) thick cubes.

Place soap in measuring cup
Place the soap into a microwave-safe glass measuring cup, such as a glass Pyrex measuring cup.

Melt soap
Microwave the soap base on a high setting for 30 seconds. Remove the measuring cup from the microwave (careful, it's hot). Using a craft stick or a spoon, stir the soap to help it melt. If necessary, heat the soap for an additional 20 seconds to melt all the soap chunks.

Watch carefully and don't let the soap simmer, which will create small bubbles that will be very hard to eliminate. Plus it will just take that much longer to let it cool back to 120°F (49°C)—the magic temperature at which you can pour it at a liquid state and not melt the other soap elements that may be a part of the project. See page 17 to learn all about layering soap.

Melt and pour soap has virtually the same weight and liquid volume. So if a project calls for 8 oz. of soap, you can melt enough soap to come up to the 8-oz. mark on the measuring cup. Easy!

EASY CLEAN UP!

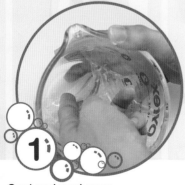

Cool and peel soap
After pouring the soap, let the leftovers coating the inside of the measuring cup cool. When the cup is cool to the touch, begin peeling along the edge. With some luck and practice, you might get it all out in one piece!

Save soap
You can use the leftover soap to remelt and use in another project. Now you can use the cup to melt more soap for a project, or put the cup in the dishwasher to clean it completely.

COLORANTS

There are a few types of colorants you can use for soap crafting. Each tutorial lists the specific type you should use to have great results. Here's a quick overview of each basic type and what makes them different.

FD&C COLORANTS

FD&C colorants are what you'll most likely find at your local craft store. These look like liquid food colors and are practically the same, but not edible. They produce gorgeous, crystal-clear colors and can be mixed to create many shades, much like watercolor paint. But be warned: You can't use them for multi-colored soaps because the colors will "bleed" together, or get blurry, after sitting for a while. Sometimes you'll see the bleeding after only a day or so.

MICAS

Micas are made of little powdery flakes that are dyed. Some bleed and some do not. They are shimmery and sometimes even sparkly. Micas come in many colors and some are iridescent (dyed a different color on each side). It is really fun to see all of the options available. Micas come as a powder, so you need to dilute them before adding them to the soap base so you don't get lumps. Follow the directions for adding powder colorants (on page 13) to add micas to your project.

TECHNIQUE:
ADDING LIQUID COLORANTS

1

Add liquid colorant
After the soap is melted, add one drop of the liquid colorant.

2

Blend color and soap
Using a craft stick, stir the melted soap and color to blend.

3

Continue for desired color
To achieve the desired color, continue stirring and adding the colorant.

OXIDES AND PIGMENTS

The most stable, nonbleeding colorants you can get fall into this category. They come in powdered form that need to be diluted in alcohol before adding to soap, or prediluted in glycerin as a liquid colorant. The liquids are by far the easiest to use and you get even more color options because many companies get creative and offer color mixtures. One important thing to note is that oxides and pigments are often opaque, but some create translucent colors. Do some tests to see how your colorants look. See the directions on page 13 for adding oxides and pigments to soap.

SOAP GLITTER—NOT A COLORANT, BUT FUN TO HAVE

Before I began soap crafting I never used glitter, but once I got inspired by everything cute and colorful, glitter became a staple in my toolbox!

Only use glitters that are specifically for soap crafting. Many other crafting glitter particles are huge and would be extremely scratchy on the skin. Even soap glitter should be used very lightly and the soap should only be used for hands, never for the face.

That said, you will find many beautiful colors and types of soap glitter available. There's even a shredded kind with an icy look that's really pretty. Soap glitter is often available in craft stores where other soap crafting supplies are found.

To add glitter to any soap: Take a pinch of glitter and use a craft stick to stir it directly into the melted soap base.

TECHNIQUE:
ADDING POWDER MICAS,
OXIDES & PIGMENTS

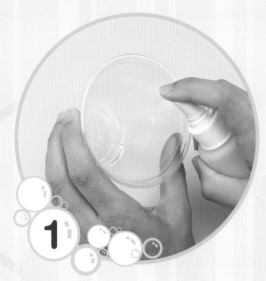

Spray alcohol
Spray some alcohol into a cup (about 10 pumps).

Add powder
Using a craft stick, add a tiny bit of powdered mica, oxide or pigment (here I'm using a pearl mica).

Mix alcohol and powder
Using the craft stick, mix the alcohol and powder together until there are no lumps.

Mix color and soap
Pour the color mixture into the melted soap base. Using the craft stick, stir the color and soap to mix well.

FRAGRANCE OILS

One of the most exciting parts of making soap is choosing the fragrance. The options are practically infinite. You can find everything from tangy lemon to s'more scents. My favorite is strawberry jam, but pretty much anything that has the word *candy* in it will wind up in my fragrance box.

When shopping for fragrance oils (commonly referred to as FOs), make sure they are specifically for soap making. Do not use FOs you buy from the grocery store intended for candles or extracts.

Fragrance oils are different than essential oils (EOs). EOs are derived from plants and are totally natural. They are nice for soap crafting, too. Some people use them exclusively.

The only drawbacks of EOs are:

☆ There are a limited number of options.

☆ They can be volatile, which means they can quickly evaporate if your soap is too hot.

I prefer FOs since they're very stable, inexpensive and come in hundreds of scents.

In glycerin soap crafting, there are just a couple of things you need to know about FOs. If the oil has a color (many are yellow), it may tint the soap. For example, if you are making white soap, the fragrance oil can turn it a creamy color. Or if you're making red soap, the FO may turn it orange. To avoid this, look for oils that are almost clear or avoid using yellow FOs in soap colors that might change.

Many FOs contain vanilla, which will gradually turn the soap brown. When shopping for FOs, check to see if it will discolor. If so, you need to buy a "vanilla color stabilizer." This is a clear additive you add in the same amount as the FO. For example: ½ tsp. (2.5mL) FO and ½ tsp. (2.5mL) stabilizer. This will stop any discoloration.

TECHNIQUE: ADDING FRAGRANCE

Measure and add fragrance
After melting and coloring the soap, add the fragrance oil to the melted soap base. The general rule is to add ½ tsp. (2.5mL) per pound of melted soap. You may use more or less depending on your personal preference.

1

2

Stir thoroughly
Using a craft stick, stir the fragrance in thoroughly.

MOLDS

One of the coolest things about melt and pour soap is that it takes the form of anything you pour it into, so there are so many options! But, whatever you choose, make sure it's flexible, like plastic and silicone, so you can unmold the soap. Glass and metal are not good choices!

Each tutorial has instructions on how and when to unmold your soap, since different types of molds behave differently. You can find any number of molds at your local craft store or online—from the basics to the funky and fun ones!

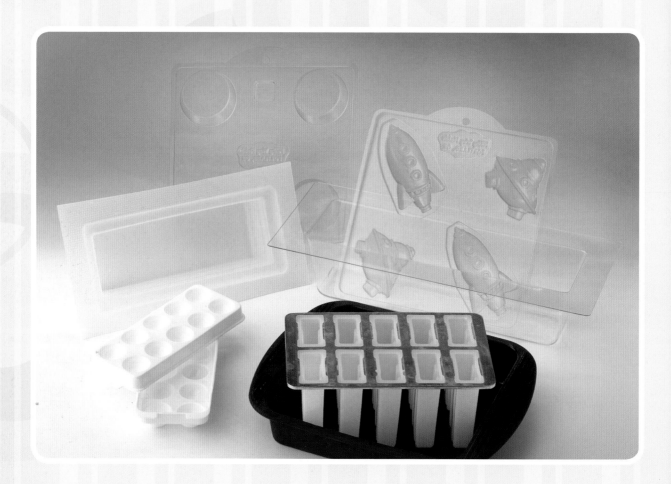

TECHNIQUE: LAYERING SOAPS

Spray alcohol
Melt the soap base for the next layer of soap, adding any desired colors and fragrances. Let the melted soap cool to 120°F (49°C). Using a spray bottle filled with rubbing alcohol, spray the surface of the hardened soap in the mold.

Pour layer
Pour the melted soap into the mold.

Spray alcohol
Spray the newly poured layer of soap with rubbing alcohol. This will pop any surface bubbles.

Take its temperature
In some cases, using a thermometer is very important to make sure the soap is cool enough to pour. The best temperature for layering soaps is 120°F (49°C).

Cooling soaps
If the soap is too hot and you want it to cool off faster, slowly pour the soap from one measuring cup to another. The slow pour with a thin stream will help cool it down faster.

FINISHING SOAPS

CUTTING SOAPS

One way to make your soaps unique is to cut them by hand into bars or by using cookie or fondant cutters. These methods make clean shapes and can reveal the layers in a new way.

The basic process is to first unmold the soap onto a cutting board. If the cutting board has a textured surface, you may want to cut it on a sheet of wax paper instead. The soap is very sensitive, so any roughness will mar the surface. If you want square or rectangular bars, cut the soap with a sharp, unserrated knife. If you want decorative shapes, you can use cookie cutters.

For really clean cuts and evenly sized bars of soap, follow the basic directions on the page 19.

PACKAGING AND WRAPPING

Glycerin is a humectant, which means it draws moisture from the air. This is why glycerin soap is considered moisturizing, which is great. The downside is that the soap will draw moisture to itself when left unwrapped, causing glycerin "sweat" to form. You can prevent this by immediately wrapping the soaps when they're done, or put them into a sealed bag or storage container until you're ready to package them.

Great choices for wrapping are stretch plastic film (like Saran Wrap), plastic treat bags or shrink film. Don't use paper because it will adhere to the soap surface. If you like the look of paper, you can wrap the soap in plastic first, then in paper.

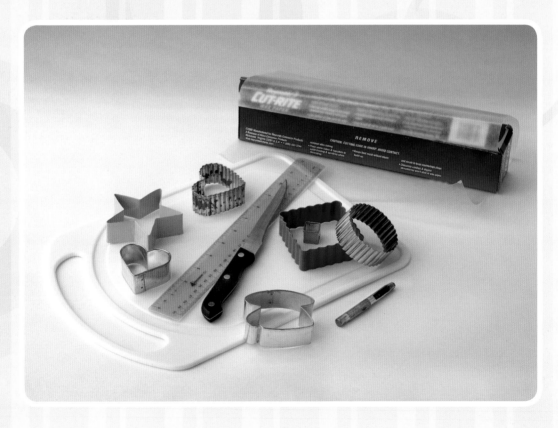

TECHNIQUE: CUTTING SOAP BARS

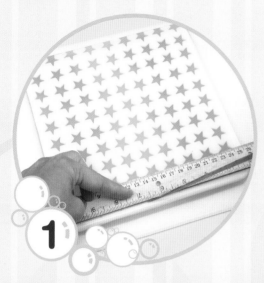

Score edges
Before cutting into bars, you'll want to trim off the edges. Using a knife and a ruler, score the guidelines.

Trim edges
Using the knife, start with a shallow cut along one of the original score lines, and make each cut deeper until you reach the cutting board. Repeat this step for all sides of the soap sheet.

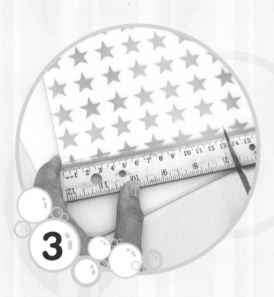

Score bar lines
Using the ruler, measure the soap into even pieces and make a mark where you want to cut. Repeat for the opposite side. Use the knife and the ruler to connect the marks with shallow score lines.

Cut bars
Using the knife, make gradually deepening cuts along the scored lines to cut the bars.

cutwork

When I first began making melt and pour soap, I wanted to create stripes and squares inspired by graphic design. Since I had not seen this done before, I had to figure it out. I quickly learned that it's easy to create impressive three-dimensional designs using cutwork.

This is a method of using cookie cutters, craft knives and even leather punches to create smaller soap shapes that can be used on their own or integrated into more complicated styles. The *Star Bright Mini Soaps* (page 22) are super easy and make adorable gifts for your party guests. The *Soap Tarts* (page 28) have hand-cut "frosting" with adorable rainbow sprinkles! With a little more time you can create a landscape with cut soap elements for the *Heavenly Bar Soaps* (page 44), which will make your friends wonder, "How'd you do that?"

These cute soaps are a snap to make. There are an unlimited number of fondant and cookie cutter shapes available so the possibilities are endless! These soaps look adorable in clear treat bags tied with ribbon. Try different shapes and colors to fit party themes and give them out as party favors! This recipe can make four different colored soaps.

STAR BRIGHT MINI SOAPS

MATERIALS

2-cup (470mL) microwave-safe glass measuring cup

1 lb. (.5kg) clear soap base

4 liquid soap colorants or food coloring of your choosing (I used fuchsia, turquoise, green and yellow)

½ tsp. (2.5mL) fragrance oil of your choosing (I used tutti frutti)

plastic flat-bottomed food storage containers, one for each soap color you want to make (a 6" [15cm] square container, or something close, is a good size)

rubbing alcohol in spray bottle

knife

cutting board

metal fondant or mini cookie cutters in star shape (approx. 1½" [4cm] diameter)

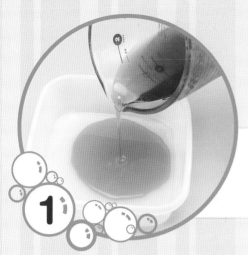

Prepare soap

In the microwave-safe glass measuring cup, melt 4 oz. (113g) of clear soap base. Add the desired color (see Technique, page 11). Stir in ⅛ tsp. (.75mL) fragrance oil (see Technique, page 15). Pour the colored soap into the food storage container to ¼" (6mm) thickness.

Add more of the color until it's a bit more intense than you really want. When the soap is cut into the thin stars, the color will be softer than it looks in the cup.

1

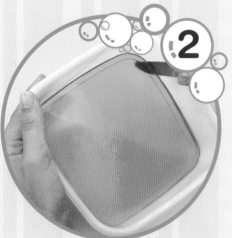

2

Unmold soap

Spray the surface of the hot soap with the rubbing alcohol to pop any surface bubbles. Allow the soap to cool on the counter for 20 minutes. Flip the container over and push on the bottom to unmold the sheet of soap. If the soap is sticking, you can pry up an edge with a knife and pull the soap out.

3

Cut soaps

Repeat steps 1 and 2 for the remaining desired colors. Place a soap sheet on the cutting board. Using the star-shaped cookie cutter, cut out the soaps. Repeat steps 1–3 for the remaining desired colors.

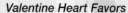

Having a hard time with the cookie cutters? Use something with a flat surface (bottom of a glass, etc.) to press the cookie cutters down. This will ensure an even press and will save your hands.

Valentine Heart Favors

It's easy to switch up colors and cutters to make mini soaps to suit any theme. Your friends will be so glad to get these sugarless treats for Valentine's Day! Use white soap base for the white and pink hearts, and clear soap base for the red hearts. Any colorant will work since you don't have to worry about colors bleeding together.

Glycerin soap is so easy to cut. Any design is possible, even really detailed ones if you have some patience. This soap was inspired by a beautiful hand-painted silhouette of my friend's daughter. You can create this look with any silhouette you like! This project makes four bars.

CAMEO BARS

MATERIALS

2-cup (470mL) microwave-safe glass measuring cup

4 oz. (113g) ultra clear soap base

black oxide soap pigment

4-cavity rectangular soap mold with flat surface

pencil or cameo design print out

cutting board

craft knife

toothpick

rubbing alcohol in spray bottle

½ lb. (226g) white soap base

¼ tsp. (1.25mL) lavender fragrance oil

Prepare soap

In the microwave-safe glass measuring cup, melt 4 oz. (113g) of the ultra clear soap base. Add the oxide (see Technique, page 13). Add more pigment mixture if needed to get a nice, dark black color. Pour the mixture into the soap mold, making a ⅛"–¼" (3mm–6mm) layer in each cavity.

Cut out cameo

Allow the soap to set to room temperature. Put the mold in the freezer for 5 minutes until the soap is solid. Meanwhile, prepare the cameo design. Using the soap mold as a size guide, draw a design or shrink a printout. Invert the soap mold and pop out the black soap. Place the design on top of the soap onto the cutting board. Use the craft knife to cut around the edge of the design and through the soap. Save any extra soap to remelt for future projects.

> Don't trust your cutting skills? Polymer clay cutters also work well.

Smooth edges with finger
Use your fingertip to smooth any rough cuts.

Smooth edges with toothpick
Use a toothpick to smooth the edges even more.

Set cameo

Melt 4 oz. (113g) of ultra clear soap base. Let it cool to 120ºF (49ºC). Pour the soap into the mold, ⅛" (3mm) thick. Quickly put the black cameo soap into the clear soap, face down. Spray the poured soap with rubbing alcohol to break any surface bubbles.

Finish soap

Let the soap layer cool and harden to room temperature. Be careful not to disturb the soap while it's hardening to avoid creating any surface wrinkles. Melt all of the white soap base. Stir in the fragrance oil (see Technique, page 15). Allow the melted soap to cool to 120ºF (49ºC). Spray the clear soap in the mold with rubbing alcohol. Pour in the white soap, filling the mold completely. Allow the bars to set to room temperature. Place the mold in the freezer for 5 minutes. Remove the mold from the freezer. Flip the mold over and pop out the soaps.

Sweet Cupcake Silhouettes

Everyone loves cupcakes! They're so popular you can even find adorable little cupcake cutters online. Just cut one out of white soap base and use clear soap base with pink mica for the background. A frosting scent would be perfect!

One trend I love to follow is felt food crafting. I saw a felt version of toaster pastries that had pink frosting and beaded sprinkles. It was so adorable! Plus, the use of layers showed me how well it would translate into a soap design. Instead of plastic beads, I use jojoba beads for a skin-friendly version of sugar sprinkles. This project makes four bars.

SOAP TARTS

 MATERIALS

small cup

jojoba beads in pink, red, yellow and blue

2-cup (470mL) microwave-safe glass measuring cup

12 oz. (340g) white soap base

red nonbleeding liquid soap colorant

4-cavity rectangular soap mold with flat surface

cutting board

craft knife

4 oz. (113g) ultra clear soap base

rubbing alcohol in spray bottle

yellow oxide colorant

brown oxide colorant

¼ tsp. (1.25mL) strawberry or cherry fragrance oil

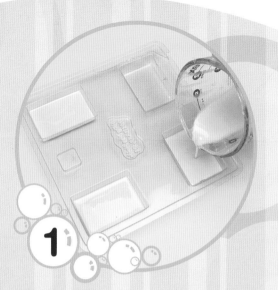

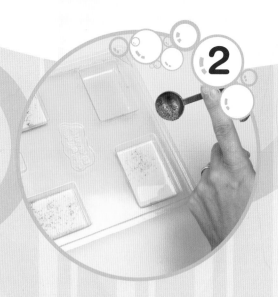

Prepare "frosting"

In a small cup, mix ½ tsp. (2.5mL) of each color jojoba beads. Set aside. In the microwave-safe glass measuring cup, melt 4 oz. (113g) of white soap base. Prepare the red colorant and add it to the soap base to get a pink color (see Technique, page 11). Pour the pink soap into each mold cavity, to ⅛" (3mm) thickness.

Add jojoba beads

Sprinkle the jojoba beads onto the soap before it solidifies.

Cut soap design

Put the mold into the freezer for 5 minutes. Remove the mold from the freezer and unmold the soaps. Put the pink soaps on the cutting board. Using the craft knife, cut curvy edges into the soap so it looks like frosting.

Set soap

Melt 4 oz. (113g) of ultra clear soap base. Allow it to cool to 120°F (49°C). Fill one mold ⅛" (3mm) deep with the ultra clear soap. Quickly spray with the rubbing alcohol and push one of the frosting soaps bead-side down into the clear soap. Repeat this step for the remaining soap mold cavities.

> Be sure to let the soap cool to 120°F (49°C). If you don't you could melt the jojoba beads.

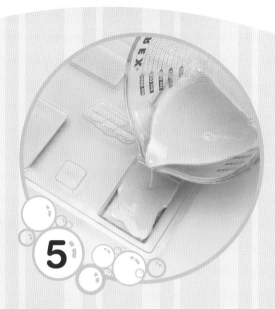

Layer soap

Spray the soap again with rubbing alcohol to pop any surface bubbles. Repeat pouring and adding the frosting for the remaining mold cavities. Now melt 8 oz. (226g) white soap base. In separate cups, prepare small amounts of the yellow and brown oxides (see Technique, page 13). Gradually add the yellow and brown colors to the melted soap until you have a good "pastry" color. Stir in the fragrance oil (see Technique, page 15). Allow the melted soap to cool to 120ºF (49ºC). Spray the soap in the mold with rubbing alcohol. Pour in the pastry soap, filling the mold completely.

Unmold soaps

Allow the soap to set to room temperature. Place the mold in the freezer for 5 minutes. Remove the mold from the freezer. To unmold the soap, invert the mold and press on the mold to pop the soaps out.

Frosted Cookie Soaps

These cute soap cookies have all the sweetness and none of the calories of the real thing! Simply use a round soap mold and white soap base for the frosting. All of the other steps are the same as the Soap Tarts. Easy peasy!

Using unusual tools for soap making is one of the things that will make your work stand out from the rest. Use a basic round leather punch to create the dotted holes for these sweet mini soaps! Use a variety of little animal cutters and combine different shapes in treat bags for very special shower favors. This recipe makes at least sixteen mini soaps.

POLKA DOT BABY SHOWER FAVORS

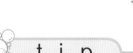

t i p

You can reuse any scraps after cutting out all of the shapes. Simply cut them up and melt them in a microwave-safe glass measuring cup. You'll get a lighter, solid color to use in another design.

MATERIALS

2-cup (470mL) microwave-safe glass measuring cup

1½ lb. (226g) white soap base

8" or 9" (20cm or 23cm) square silicone brownie pan with shiny inner surface

cutting board

circular leather punch, ¼" (6mm) diameter ("Round Hole Drive Punch")

knife

6 oz. (170g) ultra clear soap base

rubbing alcohol in spray bottle

liquid nonbleeding soap colorant in blue, red or yellow

½ tsp. (2.5mL) baby powder fragrance oil

small fondant cutters in animal shapes

Pour soap into pan

In the microwave-safe glass measuring cup, melt 8 oz. (226g) of white soap base. Pour it into the silicone pan.

Cut out dots

Allow the soap to harden. Invert the pan and remove the soap. Put the soap sheet on the cutting board, shiny side down, and use the leather punch to cut out dots.

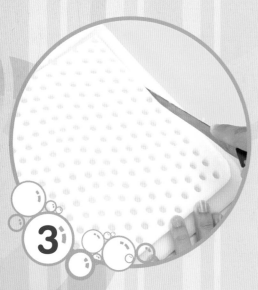

Trim soap sheet

When punching the holes, the soap actually will spread. To make sure it fits back into the mold, cut about ¼" (6mm) from two sides of the soap sheet.

Set soap

Melt 6 oz. (170g) of ultra clear soap base. Let it cool to 120ºF (49ºC). Pour it into the silicone pan. Immediately place the punched soap sheet (shiny side down) into the clear soap and use your fingers to press the soap sheet down (the soap will be hot but it won't burn you). Spray the soap with rubbing alcohol to pop any surface bubbles. Let it cool completely.

Layer soap

Melt 12 oz. (340g) of white soap base. Add the colorant (see Technique, page 11) until you have achieved a nice pastel color. Add the fragrance oil (see Technique, page 15). Let the melted soap cool to 120ºF (49ºC). Spray the surface of the hardened soap in the pan with rubbing alcohol. Pour the melted soap into the pan.

Make sure the soap thickness is not as tall as the cookie cutter.

Cut soap shapes

Allow the soap to harden. Invert the mold and unmold the soap. Place the soap sheet on the cutting board, dot side up. Use the various cutters to cut out the mini soaps.

Ice Cream Sandwich Soaps

When I had an ice cream sandwich recently, I noticed that the holes in the chocolate cookie layer would be great for the Polka Dot technique. Use clear soap base with brown oxide (a touch of black oxide is great for extra realism), then white soap base for the middle. Cut all the holes in diagonal lines. After unmolding, use a scalloped square cookie cutter to make the sandwiches.

Even really elaborate designs are possible with glycerin soap. This style uses a set of squares along with metallic mica colorants for a cool design inspired by fabrics from the seventies. This project makes a tray of soap you can cut into any number of bars.

MOD BARS

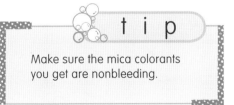

t i p

Make sure the mica colorants you get are nonbleeding.

☆ **MATERIALS**

2-cup (470mL) microwave-safe glass measuring cup

3 lb. (1.5g) ultra clear soap base

metallic mica colorants in 3 colors

8" or 9" (20cm or 23cm) square silicone brownie pan with shiny inner surface

rubbing alcohol in spray bottle

cutting board

set of 3 different sized square fondant cutters

craft stick

12 oz. (340g) white soap base

½ tsp. (2.5mL) chocolate fragrance oil

Prepare soaps

In the microwave-safe glass measuring cup, melt 8 oz. (226g) of ultra clear soap base. Add one of the mica colorants (see Technique, page 13). Add the mixture to the soap and pour into the silicone pan to ⅛"–¼" (3mm–6mm) thickness. Using the spray bottle, spray the surface with rubbing alcohol to pop any bubbles. Let the soap cool completely.

Cut soap shapes

Unmold the soap onto the cutting board. Repeat step 1 for the additional colors. Using the fondant cutters, cut the soap sheets into an assortment of square shapes. Use the smaller cutters to remove the centers of the large squares. Save any scraps for step 6.

Arrange shapes

Arrange the squares in the silicone pan in a linear pattern. When you're happy with the design, press the squares firmly to the pan to make them stick. Save any leftover shapes for step 6.

Set soap shapes

Melt 6 oz. (170g) of ultra clear soap base and let it cool to 120°F (49°C). Spray the squares in the pan with rubbing alcohol. Gently pour the melted soap to just cover the squares. If any of the squares move, use your finger or a craft stick to move them back into place.

Feeling ambitious? Try arranging the squares in a diagonal pattern—it's harder to do, but the fun design makes it worth the effort.

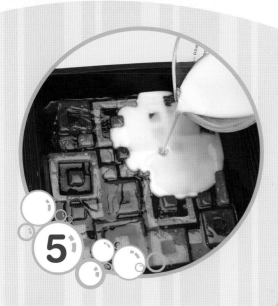

Add layer

Allow the soap to cool completely. Melt 12 oz. (340g) of white soap base. Let it cool to 120°F (49°C). Spray the hardened soap in the pan with rubbing alcohol and pour the white soap on top of it. Let the soap cool completely.

Add final layer

Melt 12 oz. (340g) of ultra clear soap base. Stir in the metallic soap scraps from steps 2 and 3 until melted. Add the fragrance oil (see Technique, page 15). Let the soap mixture cool to 120°F (49°C). Spray the hardened soap in the pan with rubbing alcohol and pour the colored soap on top.

Cut soap

Let the soap cool completely. Invert the mold and unmold the soap. See Technique, page 19, for instructions on how to cut the soap.

Use a bit of water on your finger to smooth out any imperfections after unmolding.

Combining graphic surface designs with interesting shapes allows you to create soaps to suit any style! As a child of the eighties, I have a thing for checkers, neon colors and stars. If you're like me, then this project is right up your alley. For extra inspiration, play an old mix tape while you make them. This project makes about nine star soaps.

CHECKERED STAR SOAPS

MATERIALS

2-cup (470mL) microwave-safe glass measuring cup

1½ lb. (.75kg) ultra clear soap base

black oxide soap pigment

8" or 9" (20cm or 23cm) square silicone brownie pan with shiny inner surface

small square fondant cutter, approximately ½" (1cm) wide

rubbing alcohol in spray bottle

6 oz. (170g) white soap base

nonbleeding liquid bright pink soap colorant

½ tsp. (2.5mL) cherry fragrance oil

wax paper

star-shaped cookie cutter, maximum 3" (8cm) in diameter

Prepare soap

In the microwave-safe glass measuring cup, melt 6 oz. (170g) of ultra clear soap base. Add the black oxide soap pigment to the clear soap (see Technique, page 13). Add more of the pigment mixture if needed to get a nice, dark black color. Pour the colored soap into the silicone pan.

You can add too much color! The lather of your soap should be white, even if the soap has been colored. If the lather is the color of the soap, you've gone too far! Try a lighter hand with the next batch.

Cut out checkered pattern

Let the soap set until it is firm. Unmold the soap. Use the small square cutter to cut out checkers. Keep ⅛"–¼" (3mm–6mm) of space between the rows and columns to make sure the sheet stays intact. You will be moving this so you don't want it to be too fragile.

Set soap

Melt 4 oz. (113g) of the ultra clear soap base. Pour it into the silicone pan and quickly place the checkered soap sheet into the melted soap. Use your fingers to push the soap sheet down into the pan. Spray the soap generously with rubbing alcohol to pop any surface bubbles.

Pour layer

Melt 6 oz. (170g) of white soap base. Let the melted soap cool to 120°F (49°C). Spray the soap in the mold with rubbing alcohol and pour the white soap over it.

Pour final layer

Let the white layer of soap harden completely. Melt 12 oz. (340g) of ultra clear soap base. Add the pink soap colorant (see Technique, page 11) until the soap base is hot pink. Add the fragrance oil (see Technique, page 15). Let the soap cool to 120°F (49°C). Spray the surface of the hardened white soap with rubbing alcohol and pour the pink soap on top.

Cut soap

Allow the soap to cool completely. Unmold the pan of soap. Place the soap checker side down on a piece of wax paper. Use the star-shaped cookie cutter to cut the soaps.

Use a book or drink coaster to push down the cutter if it's too hard to do with your bare hand.

Wet your finger and smooth out any fingerprints that may result from pushing the soaps out of the cutter.

Using cut soap pieces allows you to create almost anything you like—even landscapes! It's really fun to play with simple shapes. I get a lot of inspiration watching cartoons with my preschooler. This recipe makes four bars.

HEAVENLY BAR SOAPS

MATERIALS

2-cup (470mL) microwave-safe glass measuring cup

1 lb. (.5kg) white soap base

flexible loaf soap mold

½ lb. (226g) ultra clear soap base

green oxide soap pigment

cutting board

toothpick

craft knife

rubbing alcohol in spray bottle

ultramarine blue soap pigment

½ tsp. (2.5mL) milk and honey fragrance oil

ruler

unserrated knife

t i p

When buying fragrance oils, check to see if they contain any vanilla or say if they will discolor. Any fragrance oil with vanilla will discolor to brown over time, so it's good to also have some "Vanilla Color Stabilizer" in your supply box to add to any soaps you don't want to discolor.

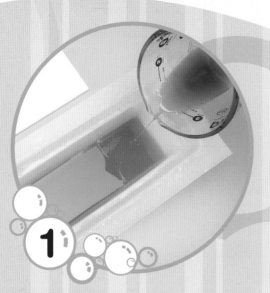

Prepare soaps

In the microwave-safe glass measuring cup, melt 4 oz. (113g) of white soap base and pour it into the loaf mold. Allow the soap to set to room temperature. Put the mold into the freezer for 5 minutes. Remove from the freezer and unmold the white soap.

Repeat this step to make a green soap sheet. This time melt 4 oz. (113g) of the ultra clear soap base and color it with the green pigment (see Technique, page 13).

Cut out designs

Place the white soap sheet on the cutting board. Use the toothpick to sketch cloud shapes into the soap sheet. When you're happy with the designs, use the craft knife to cut them out. Repeat this step for the grass, using the long side of the green soap sheet.

Use a toothpick and your finger to smooth out the edges of the clouds and the grass.

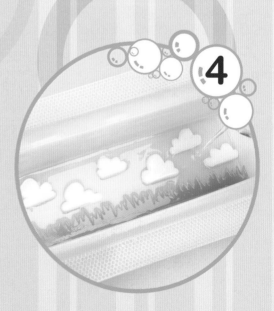

Arrange soap shapes

Place the piece of grass soap in the loaf pan along the edge and press it firmly into the pan. Arrange the soap clouds and press down.

Set soap

Melt 4 oz. (113g) of ultra clear soap base and allow it to cool to 120°F (49°C). Spray rubbing alcohol on the grass and clouds. Pour the clear soap over the shapes until they are covered.

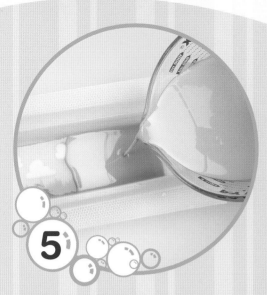

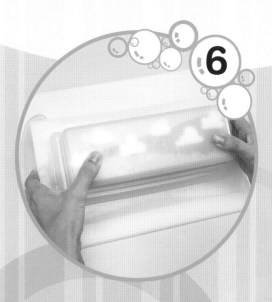

Pour layer

Allow the poured soap to set completely. Melt the remaining 12 oz. (340g) of white soap base. Color the melted soap with the ultramarine blue pigment (see Technique, page 13). Add the pigment slowly to the white soap and stir thoroughly until the desired "sky" color is achieved. Add the fragrance oil (see Technique, page 15). Allow the mixture to cool to 120°F (49°C). Spray the soap in the loaf pan with rubbing alcohol. Pour the light blue soap on top.

Unmold soap

Allow the blue soap to set until firm. To unmold the soap from the loaf pan, gently pull at the long sides of the mold. Then, turn the mold over and use your thumbs to press the soap out. If it does not release easily, place the mold in the freezer for 10 minutes, then try again.

Cut soaps

Place the soap onto the cutting board. Using the ruler, measure the soap into equal blocks. Use the unserrated knife to cut the soap into bars.

Skyline Soap Bars

A friend of mine suggested this style. While watching me make the Heavenly Bar Soaps, she was totally inspired and had lots of new ideas! We decided this one was the best. The stars are made with clear soap base and glitter, and the buildings are white with a touch of black oxide. The sky background is a beautiful shimmery midnight blue, colored with a dark blue mica. A romantic, mysterious fragrance like jasmine would be perfect for this style!

using molds creatively

One of the most readily available tools to use in glycerin soap making is the soap mold. They come in an endless assortment of shapes specifically designed for soap crafting. Glycerin soap takes detail very well and is perfectly suited to take the form of anything it's poured into or onto.

In this chapter we'll make *Martini Mix Soaps* with cocktail ice cube trays (page 50), *Alien Toy UFO Soaps* with little martian pilots inside (page 52) and yummy *Neapolitan Soapsicles* (page 56) that will make kids beg for bath time! With molds, you'll see new possibilities everywhere!

This is probably the easiest project in this whole book, and it still ranks high in the style category. Try mixing these soap dice in lots of color combinations to match your bathroom or a party theme. These little soaps are great in any kind of glass, but a martini glass is my favorite!

MARTINI MIX SOAPS

MATERIALS

2-cup (470mL) microwave-safe glass measuring cup

1 lb. (.5kg) clear soap base

pink and lime green liquid soap colorant

¼ tsp. (1.25mL) grapefruit fragrance oil, halved

mini ice cube tray (called "cubettes" or "cocktail ice cubes")

rubbing alcohol in spray bottle

tip

If your fragrance oil has a yellow tint, don't add it to the pink soap. It may change the color to orange.

Prepare soap

In the microwave-safe glass measuring cup, melt 8 oz. (226g) of clear soap base. Add the pink colorant into the soap (see Technique, page 11) until you reach the desired color. Add ⅛ tsp. (.75mL) of the grapefruit fragrance oil (see Technique, page 15). Pour the colored soap into the ice cube tray, filling it all the way up.

1

Unmold soaps

Spray the surface of the hot soap with rubbing alcohol to pop any bubbles. Allow the soap to cool on the counter for 10 minutes, then put it in the freezer for at least 15 minutes. Remove the tray from the freezer. Flex the ice cube tray to loosen the soaps.

2

Hit tray

You may need to hit the tray upside down on the counter to get out the stubborn ones. Repeat steps 1–3 for the green soaps.

The soaps will be easier to unmold if they're frozen solid, so if you have a hard time getting the dice out after 15 minutes in the freezer, put them back in the freezer for another 15.

If your soaps get a lot of condensation on them after being unmolded, let them sit out overnight or, if you're in a rush, blow them with a fan for an hour or so until the moisture disappears.

3

Primary Prisms

It's so fun to play with different color combinations for these cute little blocks. For a kids' bathroom, treat your young guests with a mix of primary colors in a jar. They'll love using a mini soap of their very own!

I'm sure you've seen the "toy in soap" concept before, but this time the toy is actually a pilot in a UFO! I love this design because it appeals to kids and there are so many different looks you can achieve by varying the spaceship color. Gold, silver, mint, pearl white and red all look great! This project makes two UFOs.

ALIEN TOY UFO SOAPS

 MATERIALS

2-cup (470mL) microwave-safe glass measuring cup

10 oz. (283g) ultra clear soap base

opalescent green mica

iridescent soap glitter

¼ tsp. (1.25mL) mint fragrance oil

Milky Way Spaceships soap mold

rubbing alcohol in spray bottle

cutting board

unserrated knife

melon baller or round metal measuring spoon

2 plastic or rubber Martian toys (these are from Oriental Trading Company, called "Out of this World Aliens," but I've seen similar ones sold as party favors, too)

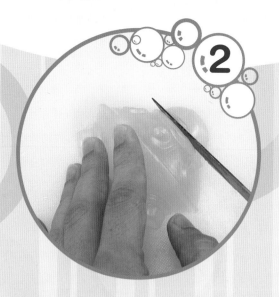

Prepare main ship body

In the microwave-safe glass measuring cup, melt 8 oz. (226g) of ultra clear soap base. Add the mica to the soap base (see Technique, page 13) until you get the desired color. Stir in a small pinch of soap glitter. Add the fragrance oil (see Technique, page 15). Pour it into the soap mold, filling to ⅛" (3mm) of the mold top.

> For other colors, use only nonbleeding micas or a combination of a pearl mica and nonbleeding colorants.

Cut out cockpit

Spray the soap in the mold with rubbing alcohol to pop any surface bubbles. Allow the soap to set to room temperature. Put the mold in the freezer for 10 minutes until the soap is solid. Invert the mold and push on the back until the soap releases. Place the soaps onto the cutting board. Use the unserrated knife to cut the "cockpit" out of the UFO. You'll leave one large piece that is the ship and one tiny piece that is the top of the ship.

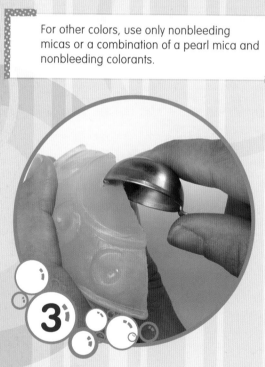

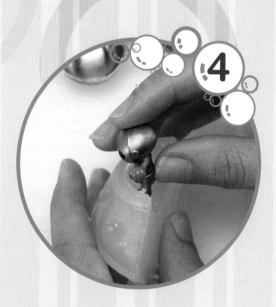

Carve out space

Using the melon baller or metal measuring spoon, scoop a cavity out of the back side of the ship body. Carve enough out so the Martian fits inside but his head sticks up into the cockpit space.

Check toy fit

Check to make sure the hollowed section is deep enough so the Martian's back doesn't stick out farther than the back side of the soap. Repeat step 3 if needed.

Position soap and toy

Put the UFO ship body back into the mold, as well as the top tip of the ship. Position the Martian in the mold as shown.

5

Set soap

Melt 2 oz. (57g) more of ultra clear soap base. Stir in a pinch of soap glitter and keep stirring until the glitter doesn't sink anymore. Lightly spray the soap in the mold with rubbing alcohol. Pour the clear soap into the cockpit cavity.

6

7

Finish soap

Allow the clear soap to completely fill the mold and cover the tip and body of the ship. Spray with rubbing alcohol to remove any surface bubbles. Let the soap harden. You should be able to pop the soap out of the mold without having to freeze it.

This style is my baby. It is easily my most popular soapsicle style. I think people love it because it is both nostalgic and classic, or maybe because everyone loves Neapolitan ice cream! Whatever it is, you will love how easy it is to make! This project makes eight 3-oz. soapsicles.

NEAPOLITAN SOAPSICLES

MATERIALS

2-cup (470mL) microwave-safe glass measuring cup

1 lb. + 2 oz. (509g) white soap base

nonbleeding liquid red soap colorant

½ tsp. (2.5mL) strawberry fragrance oil

any plastic freezer pop mold, 3-oz. (85g) capacity

rubbing alcohol in spray bottle

9 oz. (255g) clear soap base

brown oxide soap pigment

½ tsp. (2.5mL) chocolate fragrance oil

8 wooden craft sticks

small saucepan

Pour pink layer

In the microwave-safe glass measuring cup, melt 9 oz. (255g) of white soap base. Add the red colorant (see Technique, page 11) until you get a nice strawberry pink color. Add the strawberry fragrance oil (see Technique, page 15). Fill 8 pop molds ⅓ full.

Liberally spray the hot soap with rubbing alcohol after pouring each layer into the molds to remove all the bubbles. If any remain, they will be visible on the finished soaps.

Pour white layer

Allow the soap in the molds to set to room temperature. Melt 9 oz. (255g) of white soap base. Allow the melted soap to cool to 120°F (49°C). Spray the pink soap in molds with rubbing alcohol. Pour white soap in until each mold is ⅔ full.

Pour brown layer

Spray the soap in each mold with rubbing alcohol to pop any bubbles. Allow the soap in the molds to set to room temperature. Melt 9 oz. (255g) of clear soap base and add the brown pigment (see Technique, page 13). Add as much pigment mixture as needed to get a rich chocolate color. Add the chocolate fragrance oil (see Technique, page 15). Spray the white soap in each mold with rubbing alcohol. Pour the brown soap into each mold, leaving ⅛" (3mm) from the top edge.

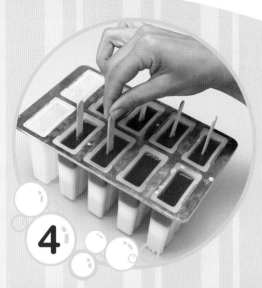

Insert sticks

Spray the tops of the brown soap with rubbing alcohol to pop any bubbles. Insert the sticks through the melted brown soap into the firmer white soap. I like to leave about 2" (5cm) sticking out of the soap.

> To make sure sticks are centered, put them in at eye level. Check the positions from the side, too, and adjust if necessary.

Separate molds

Put the molds in the freezer for 30 minutes. Remove the mold from the freezer. If you can separate the individual soap molds, do so.

Dunk mold

To unmold the soapsicles, heat up about 4 cups (940mL) of water in a small saucepan. Once it comes to a boil, take it off the heat. (If the molds do not separate, use a pot big enough for the entire mold set to be dunked altogether.) While holding onto the sticks, dunk each mold into the water for 4 seconds or so.

Unmold soap

Remove the mold from the water. Hold the soap mold over the counter. Pull on the stick to remove the soap from the mold.

These awesome rocket soaps are great because not too many soap designs appeal to boys. Plus, this soap will last a long time when hung up in the shower between uses. These rockets can be bright or retro! Try clear liquid colorants for a bright look, or metallic micas for something a bit more nostalgic. Try different color combinations and don't be afraid to use colors that bleed—the color blending is one of the great things about it! This project makes six soap rockets.

ROCKET SOAP ON A ROPE

MATERIALS

marker

empty cereal box or similar weight cardboard

scissors

6 soap ropes, looped with ends fused or knotted together

2-cup (470mL) microwave-safe glass measuring cup

1 lb. + 4 oz. (566g) clear soap base

yellow mica

½ tsp. (2.5mL) orange fragrance oil

set of rocket-shaped freezer-pop molds, 3 oz. (85g) capacity

rubbing alcohol in spray bottle

blue mica

craft stick

Create circle template

Using the marker, create a circle template on the piece of cardboard by loosely tracing around the open end of one of the rocket molds. Do this a total of 6 times.

1

2

Mark center with "X"

Using the scissors, cut out the 6 circle templates, adding approx. ½" (1cm) in width. Cut a ½" (1cm) X in the center of each circle. You might have to fold the cardboard circles to cut the X.

Insert rope

Insert the fused or knotted end of the soap rope through the center of the X.

3

Pull rope through

Pull the joined end of the rope through the X about 2" (5cm). Repeat steps 3 and 4 for all the cardboard circles and soap ropes.

Pour first layer

Set the cardboard circles aside. In the microwave-safe glass measuring cup, melt half of the clear soap base (10 oz. [283g]). Add ⅛ tsp. (.5mL) of yellow mica (see Technique, page 13). Stir until incorporated. Add the fragrance oil (see Technique, page 15). Fill each mold halfway.

Pour second layer

Spray the poured soap generously with rubbing alcohol to pop any surface bubbles. Repeat step 5 for the rest of the soap base, coloring it with the blue mica. Check the yellow soap in the molds: Once it forms a soft skin on the surface (about 15 minutes after you poured the layer), gently pour the blue soap into the molds, filling to ⅜" (1cm) from the top.

Blend colors

Using the craft stick, mix the colors where they meet, punching through the yellow soap skin to blend the layers.

7

Insert ropes

Spray the poured soap with alcohol to pop any surface bubbles. Insert the joined end of the soap rope into the soap, letting the paper circle rest on the top of the mold. Try to get the rope as centered in the rocket as you can. Repeat this step for all the soaps.

8

Unmold soaps

Allow the soap to set at room temperature. Put the molds into the freezer for 20 minutes. Remove the molds from the freezer and pull the cardboard circles off of the ropes. To unmold the soaps, squeeze the mold to loosen the soap. Pull on the rope to release the soap from the mold.

9

If the soap doesn't unmold, you can put the mold under hot running water until it comes out.

The ability to use multiple colors is one of the best things about glycerin soap crafting. These soaps are special because the second color is hidden until you make the "bite" mark! For a final dose of yumminess, sprinkle your soaps with real granulated sugar. Sweet! This project makes four soaps.

JELLY DONUT SOAPS

 MATERIALS

2-cup (470mL) microwave-safe glass measuring cup

8 oz. (226g) clear soap base

bright pink nonbleeding liquid soap colorant

purple nonbleeding liquid soap colorant

pearl mica

½ tsp. (2.5mL) fragrance oil, strawberry or grape jelly scents are favorites

basic round soap mold with 4 cavities

rubbing alcohol in spray bottle

round cookie cutter, about ½" (1cm) smaller diameter than the face of the soap mold

cutting board

12 oz. (340g) white soap base

yellow oxide colorant

brown oxide colorant

scalloped biscuit cutter

sugar (optional)

Prepare soap

In the microwave-safe glass measuring cup, melt 8 oz. (226g) of clear soap base. Add a few drops each of bright pink and purple colorant (see Technique, page 11). Add a pinch of the mica to the colored soap and stir until blended. Add the fragrance oil (see Technique, page 15). Pour the soap into each mold, filling each mold cavity halfway.

If you can get oxides dissolved in glycerin, that will make achieving tricky colors much easier. Just add color, drop by drop, until you get it.

Unmold soap

Using the spray bottle filled with rubbing alcohol, spray the poured soap to pop any surface bubbles. Let the soap harden completely. Unmold the soap onto the cutting board by turning the mold upside down and pushing on the back with your thumbs. If it's too difficult, put the mold in the freezer for 5 minutes.

Cut soap

Using the round cookie cutter, cut a smaller circle out of the soap (this will be your "jelly" filling).

If possible, choose cutters that are coated—they'll last much longer.

Pour layer

Melt 12 oz. (340g) of white soap base. Prepare a pinch of yellow oxide colorant and stir into soap (see Technique, page 13). Repeat this process for the brown oxide colorant. Add the brown and yellow colorants until you have a realistic donut color. It helps to have a real donut nearby! Pour the colored soap into molds ¼" (6mm) thick.

Finish soap

Let the donut-colored soap harden. Place the jelly soap disk on top of the hardened soap in the mold. Spray the soaps with rubbing alcohol. Top off each mold with the donut-colored soap. (You may need to reheat the soap if it has hardened. Make sure it has cooled to 120ºF [49ºC] before pouring it over the jelly soap.)

Unmold soap

Spray the soap with rubbing alcohol to pop any surface bubbles. Allow it to cool completely. Unmold the soaps by turning the mold over and pushing on the center of the soaps. Using the biscuit cutter, cut a "bite" out of the soap, revealing the jelly middle. If desired, dust the soaps with sugar for a realistic finish!

Cream-Filled Chocolate Cake Soaps

A trip to the gas station could be an amazing source of inspiration! These chocolaty treats are loved by everyone, and it's so easy to make a soapy version. Use white soap base for the cream center, and clear soap base colored with brown and black oxides for the outside. You'll love cutting into them when you're finished!

67

A throwback to days of plastic lunch boxes and cartons of chocolate milk, these loaf soaps feature the primary colored bubbles we know and love from white bread packages. The mold to make the colored spheres is actually an ice ball tray I found in a Japanese housewares store. (But when I went online I found them under "Golf Ball Ice Cube Tray." Golf ball ice cubes? Go figure!) Any mold that makes spheres around 1" (3cm) in diameter will be great for this project.

WONDER BARS

 MATERIALS

4-cup (940mL) microwave-safe glass measuring cup

1½ lb. (226g) clear soap base

blue, bright yellow and red nonbleeding liquid soap colorants

1½ tsp. (2.5mL) strawberry jam fragrance oil

ball ice tray, with 1" (3cm) diameter cavities

rubber bands

1½ lb. (226g) white soap base

40 oz. (1.25kg) soap loaf mold (or smaller, but you won't need as much soap)

rubbing alcohol in spray bottle

cutting board

unserrated knife

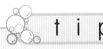 **t i p**

My favorite thing about this design is that when you cut the loaf, all the dots will be in different sizes, which is just like the old white bread graphic! Plus, as you use the soap, the dots will get smaller or bigger. It's so cool!

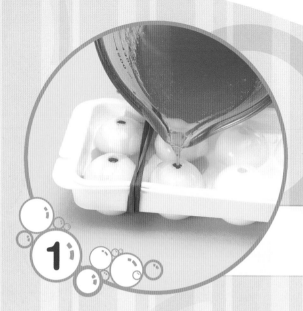

Prepare colored balls

In the microwave-safe glass measuring cup, melt 8 oz. (226g) of clear soap base. Add the red colorant until you get a nice bright color (see Technique, page 11). Add ¼ tsp. (1.25mL) of fragrance oil (see Technique, page 15). Assemble the ball mold. Use rubber bands to hold the mold together. Pour the melted red soap into the holes.

It may get messy and that's OK! To make the pouring easier, I had to drill my holes to make them bigger.

1

Repeat for additional colors

Allow the soap to set to room temperature. Put the mold in the freezer for 20 minutes until solid. Remove the mold from the freezer. Unmold the soap by pulling the trays apart. Turn the mold upside down, and gently press the mold with your thumbs. You may need to gently tap the mold upside down on a table to loosen the balls. Repeat steps 1 and 2 for the yellow and blue colored balls.

2

Begin layering

Melt 16 oz. (453g) of white soap base. Allow it to cool to 120°F (49°C). Pour the melted soap into the loaf mold about ½" (1cm) deep. Place the red balls into the poured soap in a row along one side of the mold, about ½" (1cm) apart.

3

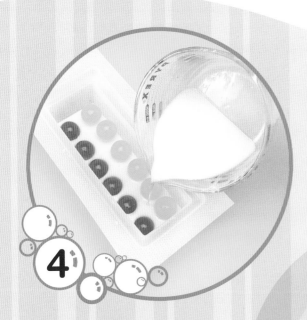

Add yellow layer

Spray rubbing alcohol on the poured soap and red soap balls. Allow the poured soap to set to room temperature. If the remaining white soap in the measuring cup has set, warm it up again to completely melt it. Spray the soap in the mold with rubbing alcohol. Place the yellow balls in a row opposite the red balls, about ½" (1cm) apart. Pour the soap into the mold, covering the red balls completely. You may now be out of white soap. Melt the remaining white soap base.

4

Add blue layer

Allow the soap in the mold to set. Repeat step 4 for the blue balls, which will now be placed over the red ones. To create a more random pattern, place the blue balls between the yellow ones.

5

Pour soap

Spray the soap in the mold with rubbing alcohol. Fill the mold with white soap, covering the yellow balls completely.

6

Add final layer

You will have a few balls of each color left over. Randomly place the balls onto the set soap surface. Spray rubbing alcohol on the soaps in the mold. Fill the mold with the remaining white soap, halfway up the last soap balls.

7

Unmold soap

Spray the soap with rubbing alcohol to pop any surface bubbles. Let the soap set completely. Unmold the soap by pulling the sides away from the soap, then pushing the mold from the bottom.

If the loaf mold won't release the soap, stick it in the freezer for 10 minutes, then try again.

8

Cut bars

Place the soap loaf onto the cutting board. Using the sharp unserrated knife, cut the soap loaf into bars approximately ¾" (2cm) thick.

9

Bubble Bars

When I was thinking about different versions of the Wonder Bar, I realized how much they look like bubbles! Pearl mica is a great colorant and creates the iridescent look I wanted. Use it with clear soap base to make the balls, then use white soap base with nonbleeding blue colorant for the bar. Just make sure you mix all the light blue soap you'll need for the whole loaf before you start. It's always hard to match a color after you've run out!

color techniques

Color is the most exciting part of glycerin soap crafting! When I first got started, I was amazed at all of the possibilities. Not only can you create any color imaginable—from neons to soft pastels—you can also have clarity, opacity and shimmer to add dimension to your designs.

In this chapter we'll swirl colors in the *Marbled Soap Cones* (page 76), create a kaleidoscope effect with the *Floating Dots Bars* (page 86), and even design *Plaid Soaps* (page 94)! These projects will show you how to combine colorful effects to create eye-popping styles.

Unmold soap

Allow the soap to harden completely. Unmold the soap by turning the pan of soap onto your hand and peeling away the pan.

Cut soap

With the marbled side down on the sheet of wax paper, use the cookie cutter to cut out the cone shapes.

Having trouble pushing down the cookie cutter? Use a block of wood or a flat-bottomed glass to help push it down evenly.

Hot Chocolate Bars

When the days get chilly, something about a mug of hot chocolate is so therapeutic! These swirly soaps make me think of whipped cream stirred into rich chocolate. To make them, marble the white soap base with clear soap base colored with cappuccino mica. Add a solid layer of white soap (which really shows off the swirls), then cut the soap into shapes with a cute mug or cup cutter. Check out all of the wonderful chocolate scents available. Yum!

If you've ever owned a pair of high-tops, you'll have to try this design. The star pattern is cool on its own, but what's even better is that the stars are windows to a two-tone, blended-stripe background. It's a lot easier than it looks—but don't tell your friends that. Let them be impressed! This project makes one large pan of soap that you can cut into any number of bars.

STAR BARS

MATERIALS

2 2-cup (470mL) microwave-safe glass measuring cups

6 oz. (170g) white soap base

8" or 9" (20cm or 23cm) square silicone brownie pan, with shiny inner surface

cutting board

mini polymer star cutter, approximately ¾" (2cm) in diameter

ruler or straightedge (optional)

pencil (optional)

2½ lb. (2.25g) ultra clear soap base

rubbing alcohol in spray bottle

bright yellow and bright green nonbleeding colorants

½ tsp. (2.5mL) pineapple fragrance oil

Pour soap
In one of the microwave-safe glass measuring cups, melt all of the white soap base. Pour the melted soap into the silicone pan.

Unmold soap
Allow the soap to harden. Unmold the soap by peeling away a side of the pan and pulling out the soap sheet.

Cut out stars
Place the soap sheet onto the cutting board. Using the star cutter, cut out rows of stars, leaving about ¼" (6mm) in between each star to keep the sheet intact.

You may want to use a ruler or straightedge to help keep the rows of stars lined up. Just use a pencil to draw the guides. Place the side you have drawn on face-up in the pan for step 4.

When the star cutter gets full, use the end of a pen to push out the soap.

4

Set soap layer
Melt 6 oz. (170g) of ultra clear soap base. Allow the soap to cool to 120ºF (49ºC). Pour the clear soap into the pan. Quickly press the star-cut soap sheet into the clear soap, pushing it down to the bottom of the pan.

Pour yellow soap

Using the spray bottle with rubbing alcohol, spray the soap to pop any surface bubbles. Allow the soap to cool to room temperature.

Melt half of the remaining ultra clear soap base. Add the bright yellow colorant (see Technique, page 11). Add ¼ tsp. (1.25mL) of fragrance oil (see Technique, page 15). Repeat, using the separate measuring cup, and color with the bright green colorant and the remaining ¼ tsp. (1.25mL) of fragrance oil.

Allow both cups of soap to cool to 120°F (49°C). Spray the soap in the pan with rubbing alcohol. Pour all the yellow soap on top.

Pour green soap

Pour the green soap into the yellow soap along 2 sides, creating a stripe pattern.

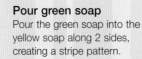

Unmold and cut

Spray the soap with rubbing alcohol to pop any surface bubbles. Allow the soap to harden. Unmold the soap by flipping the pan over a cutting board and peeling the pan off the soap. See Technique, page 19, for information on how to cut the soap into bars.

Cut with the star side up to
see the pattern when cutting.

Candy Bars

As you might be able to tell, my two favorite
shapes are stars and hearts. This lovely version of
the Star Bars uses a tiny heart polymer clay cutter
and stripes of hot pink and purple. Fragrance with
any pink candy scent you like. So cute!

85

These are not your typical polka dots—they're amazing glassy floating dots that shine through each other like a kaleidoscope! The ability to layer elements gives glycerin soap a dimension you can't find in any other craft, and this soap features it with fun and style. This project makes one large tray of soap that you can cut into any number of bars.

FLOATING DOTS BARS

t i p

Mixing dot sizes would also be really fun!

I don't recommend using any fragrance for this style since it is primarily clear and you don't want it to yellow from any fragrance oils.

MATERIALS

2-cup (470mL) microwave-safe glass measuring cup

3 lb. (1.5kg) ultra clear soap

blue, yellow and orange nonbleeding liquid colorants

8" or 9" (20cm or 23cm) square silicone brownie pan with shiny inner surface

cutting board

circular polymer cutter, approximately 1" (3cm) in diameter

3 cereal bowls or similar containers

rubbing alcohol in spray bottle

Begin making dots

Using the microwave-safe glass measuring cup, melt 6 oz. (170g) of ultra clear soap base. Color with 2-3 drops of the yellow colorant until you have a color that is bright but not totally opaque (See Technique, page 11). Pour the melted soap into the silicone pan. Let the soap harden. Unmold the soap by bending back a corner of the pan and pulling the soap out with your fingers. Repeat this step for the blue and orange soaps.

Cut out dots

Place the soap sheet on the cutting board. Using the circular cutter, cut lots of dots from each soap sheet.

t i p

If a seam of a cookie cutter is starting to split, cover the seam with a piece of cellophane tape to extend the life of the cutter.

Set aside a few dots of each color and cut them in half. These can help fill in any gaps that may be created around the edges of the pan.

Begin dot layer

Mix the colored soap dots and divide them evenly into the 3 bowls. Melt 8 oz. (226g) of ultra clear soap base. Allow the melted soap to cool to 120ºF (49ºC). Pour the melted soap into the silicone pan. Spray the soap with rubbing alcohol to pop any surface bubbles. Quickly place the dots from one bowl, creating a random design in the clear soap.

3

4

Add 2 more dot layers

Spray the soap again with the alcohol to remove any bubbles. Allow the soap to form a thick skin. It does not need to set up completely. Spray the surface of the soap with rubbing alcohol and repeat step 3 to create 2 more layers of dots (don't feel like you have to use all the dots). Melt the remaining soap base. After the final soap layer has cooled, pour the melted soap into the mold.

Unmold and cut into bars

Allow the entire pan of soap to harden. Unmold the soap by flipping the mold over a cutting board and peeling the mold away. See Technique, page 19, to learn about cutting the soap into bars.

5

It's pretty hard to find a soap project that appeals to people with an edgy style, but this one will please even your toughest friends! The flames fade from red to orange and are set off by a vivid yellow background. This project makes four bars.

FLAME BARS

MATERIALS

2-cup (470mL) microwave-safe glass measuring cup

1 lb. (.5kg) clear soap base

red and orange nonbleeding liquid colorants

iridescent soap glitter

4-cavity basic rectangular soap mold

cutting board

knife

craft stick

craft knife

yellow mica

½ tsp. (2.5mL) fragrance oil (cinnamon would be appropriate)

rubbing alcohol in spray bottle

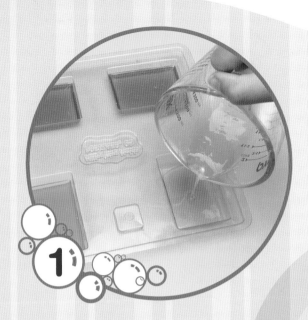

Prepare soap

Using the microwave-safe measuring cup, melt 4 oz. (113g) of clear soap base. Stir in red colorant to achieve an intense shade (see Technique, page 11). Add a pinch of soap glitter and mix. Fill 2 of the mold cavities halfway. Repeat this step using the orange colorant.

Chop soaps

Allow the soap to set to room temperature. Place the mold in the freezer for 10 minutes. Remove the mold from the freezer and unmold all the soaps. Place the soaps on the cutting board. Using the knife, chop the soaps into small pieces.

Divide soap pieces

Fill each of the mold cavities with the pieces of soap, placing red pieces on one side of the mold cavity and orange pieces on the other.

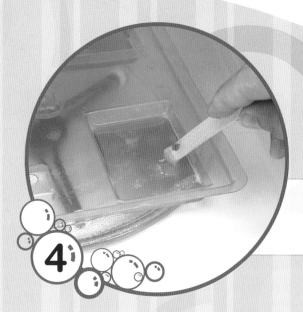

Blend soap

Put the mold into the microwave and heat for 15 seconds. While keeping the mold in the microwave, use the craft stick to gently blend the soaps where they meet.

If you have a smaller microwave that has a turntable, be sure to buy a mold that will fit in the microwave and allow it to turn for an even heating.

4

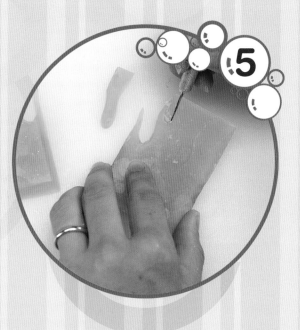

5

Cut soap

Leave the mold in the microwave until the soap is solid. Put the mold in the freezer for 10 minutes. Unmold the soaps. Using the craft knife, cut a flame design into the orange side of each soap. For a smoother cut, make gradual cuts into the soap.

Unsure of the design? Use a toothpick and trace a design on the back of the bar before cutting it out. When you're satisfied with the design, use the craft knife to cut away the pieces.

6

Set soap

Melt 8 oz. (226g) of the clear soap base. Stir in a small amount of yellow mica until well blended (see Technique, page 13). Add the fragrance oil (see Technique, page 15). Allow the melted soap to cool to 120ºF (49ºC). Complete one bar at a time in this manner: Fill the mold cavity with a ⅛" (3mm) layer of yellow soap, then place the flame soap into the mold.

Finish bar

If it's needed, spray the soap in the mold with rubbing alcohol. Continue filling the mold with yellow soap.

7

8

Unmold soaps

Repeat the final part of step 6 and step 7 until all the molds are filled. Spray the soaps with rubbing alcohol as needed. Allow the soaps to harden. Unmold the soaps.

Of all the soaps I have made, this one gets the most oohs and aahs, and also questions about how I did it. The secret is to have a light hand when coloring the soap used for the stripes. Although nonbleeding colorants can be very opaque, they can also be very sheer, which is crucial for this style. Scalloped biscuit cutters make excellent soap cutters since they are extra deep, very durable and appropriately sized. This project makes approximately nine scalloped rounds.

PLAID SOAPS

MATERIALS

2-cup (470mL) microwave-safe glass measuring cup

1 lb. + 14 oz. (850g) ultra clear soap base

blue, yellow and pink nonbleeding liquid colorants

8" or 9" (20cm or 23cm) square silicone brownie pan

cutting board

knife

ruler or straightedge

rubbing alcohol in spray bottle

12 oz. (340g) white soap base

½ tsp. (2.5mL) lemon fragrance oil, or any scent you like

wax paper

scalloped biscuit cutter, approximately 2½" (6cm) in diameter

Prepare soap

In the microwave-safe glass measuring cup, melt 6 oz. (170g) of the ultra clear soap base. Add one drop of blue colorant at a time, stirring thoroughly until you get a sheer color (see Technique, page 11). Pour the colored soap into the silicone pan. Let the soap harden. Unmold the soap. Repeat this step for the yellow and pink soap sheets.

Cut soap into strips

Place a soap sheet on the cutting board. Using the ruler or the straightedge and the knife, cut the colored soap sheets into random widths of strips. Exact widths are not important, since a mix is really nice for this design. Repeat this step for all of the soap sheets.

Plan design

You will need to lay the strips quickly for the next steps, so take a moment to plan the plaid pattern. Alternate colors and widths, with about ¼" (6mm) between each strip. Lay them in one direction, then crosswise. Once you have decided how you want the pattern to look, carefully put the strips aside.

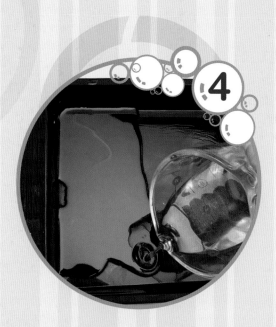

Prepare soap layer

Melt 6 oz. (170g) of the ultra clear soap base. Pour it into the pan.

5

Place strips

Lay the first set of strips into the hot soap. Press the strips into the soap. Using the spray bottle with rubbing alcohol, spray the soap to pop any surface bubbles. Allow the soap to cool to room temperature.

If the clear soap starts forming a skin before you're done laying the strips, spray the soap liberally with rubbing alcohol to dissolve the skin.

6

Pour another layer

Melt 6 oz. (170g) of ultra clear soap base. Spray the soap in the pan with rubbing alcohol. Pour the clear soap into the pan.

7

Place second layer of strips

Lay the second set of strips, in the opposite direction, into the soap.

Pour layer

Let the soap in the mold cool to room temperature. Melt 12 oz. (340g) of white soap base. Add the fragrance oil (see Technique, page 15). Allow the melted soap to cool to 120°F (49°C). Spray the plaid soap in the pan with rubbing alcohol. Pour the white soap over the plaid soap.

8

9

Unmold soap

Let the soap harden. Unmold the soap by flipping the mold over and peeling the mold away.

Cut soap

Turn the soap plaid side down onto the wax paper. Using the scalloped biscuit cutter, cut out the soap.

You should cut these with the plaid side down so you don't get any fingerprints on the beautiful face of the soap when you push each round out of the cutter. If you'd prefer to be able to see the design as you cut, you can always use water to smooth out the fingerprints later.

10

Glittery Gingham Heart Soaps
The plaid technique is beautiful when only one color is used, too. Try this all-American look with strips of clear soap colored with nonbleeding red and a pinch of soap glitter. Cut them into heart shapes for a pretty Valentine's Day gift!

99

unusual
tools &
materials

Melting and pouring
is just the tip of the iceberg!
Glycerin soap is an amazingly sculptural
medium and can perform beautifully with
techniques borrowed from other crafts.

It can be molded like polymer clay for
the *Waffle Sandwich Hearts* (page 110),
melted like chocolate for the *Crazy
Circles Soaps* (page 114) and carved
like clay for the *Maple Bars* (page
122). Using unusual tools for your
soaps will result in truly
unique creations!

A secret that cake decorators know is the way fondant picks up texture from other surfaces. The same is true for glycerin soap. Simply find a material with an interesting raised design, place it in a pan, and pour melted soap over it. Just peel the fabric off after unmolding and you have a brand-new texture! This project reminds me of having lemon cookies in my grandma's kitchen. I probably could have found this material there, too—it's a vinyl lace tablecloth! This makes approximately sixteen soaps.

LACEY LEMON COOLERS

MATERIALS

vinyl lace tablecloth or placemat

scissors

8" or 9" (20cm or 23cm) square silicone brownie pan with shiny inner surface

cellophane tape

2-cup (470mL) microwave-safe glass measuring cup

2 lb. (1kg) white soap base

craft stick

nonbleeding bright yellow liquid soap colorant

½ tsp. (2.5mL) lemon fragrance oil

rubbing alcohol in spray bottle

cutting board

scalloped heart cutter, approximately 2" (5cm) in diameter

Prepare lace pattern
Using the scissors, trim the vinyl lace tablecloth or placemat to fit the bottom of the silicone pan. Place the piece pattern side up in the pan. Using the cellophane tape, secure the corners of the vinyl piece to the pan.

Pour layer
In the microwave-safe glass measuring cup, melt 8 oz. (226g) of white soap base. Pour the melted soap over the vinyl. If the center of the vinyl starts to float to the surface, use a craft stick to push it back down.

Pour yellow layer
Allow the soap to harden. Melt the remaining white soap base. Add the yellow colorant until you have a nice light lemon color (see Technique, page 11). Add the fragrance oil (see Technique, page 15). Allow the soap to cool to 120ºF (49ºC). Using the spray bottle filled with rubbing alcohol, spray the white soap in the pan. Pour the yellow soap on top.

Unmold soap
Let the soap harden. Unmold the soap by flipping the mold over and peeling the mold away. It will most likely look messy, but don't worry.

4

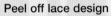

Peel off lace design
Place the soap sheet on the cutting board. Find a corner of the vinyl and peel it off of the soap sheet.

5

Cut soaps
Using your fingers, gently pick off any large chunks of soap from the surface of the soap sheet. Using the heart cutter, cut out the soaps.

6

Polymer clay artists have an amazing material for creating mini molds quickly and easily called Elasticlay. It is soft clay that takes detail perfectly and bakes flexible. For this project, we're using a foam block stamp with an ice cream theme and making a texture sheet with the Elasticlay. You'll be able to use this sheet over and over!

ICE CREAM BARS

MATERIALS

Sculpey Elasticlay

ceramic tile or glass pie plate

small rolling pin

any small, flat-bottomed plastic container approximately 6" × 6" (15cm × 15cm) and 1" (3cm) deep

knife

foam block stamp with ice cream designs

small amount of flour

2-cup (470mL) microwave-safe glass measuring cup

approximately 8 oz. (226g) white soap base (see step 4 to determine exact amount)

bright pink or red liquid soap colorant (does not need to be nonbleeding)

¼ tsp. (1.25mL) strawberry fragrance oil

rubbing alcohol in spray bottle

cutting board

butter knife (optional)

scalloped square cookie cutter or your favorite shape

Roll out Elasticlay

On the ceramic tile or the bottom of the glass pie plate, use the small rolling pin to roll out the Elasticlay to ¼" (6mm) thickness. If the Elasticlay gets sticky, put it in the freezer for 3 minutes to stiffen it.

Cut Elasticlay

Press the bottom of the plastic container into the clay; it will leave an indent. Using the knife, cut the Elasticlay slightly smaller than the impression of the bottom of the plastic container.

Stamp clay

Dip the foam block stamp in the flour and shake off the excess. Stamp the clay with the various designs.

Avoid using any stamps with words because the words will come out backward! I didn't use the side of this stamp that says "Sweet" because I knew it would turn out wrong.

Measure soap

Bake the clay according to the package directions. Allow it to cool. To determine how much soap to melt, pour water into the plastic container to ¾" (2cm) deep. Empty the water into the microwave-safe glass measuring cup and note the measurement. (In this case, I measured 8 oz. [226g].)

Soap's weight and volume are almost the same, so if you measured 8 liquid oz. of water to fill the mold, you can weigh out 8 oz. of soap and it will be really close.

Pour layer

In the microwave-safe glass measuring cup, melt enough white soap base to match the measurement from step 4. Add the colorant to make a pink color (see Technique, page 11). Add the fragrance oil (see Technique, page 15). Place the baked clay stamped side up into the container. Pour the melted soap on top of the Elasticlay.

Unmold soap

Spray the soap in the mold with rubbing alcohol. Let the soap harden. Unmold the soap by flipping the mold over and pushing on the bottom of the mold. Place the soap sheet on the cutting board. Peel the texture sheet off of the soap. You may need to use a butter knife to pry an edge out of the soap before peeling it off completely.

Cut soaps
Using the desired cookie cutter, cut the soap into various shapes.

7

Make the most of your soap: Arrange the cookie cutters before you cut out the shapes to maximize the number of soaps you can get.

Birthday Party Soap
Foam stamps are so popular that you're bound to find many tempting options at your local craft store or online. For this cute style I found a set of coordinating stamps in a birthday theme. Bright yellow reminds me of buttercream frosting, so I used a birthday cake scent. Your party guests will love washing up with this soap next to your sink!

I love dessert, as you can probably tell, and when I saw a waffle and ice cream sandwich online, I was inspired! This project uses the Elasticlay again, but we create a totally new texture with some simple tools. The heart shape adds an extra dose of cuteness!

WAFFLE SANDWICH HEARTS

 MATERIALS

ceramic tile or glass pie plate

small rolling pin

Sculpey Elasticlay (8 oz. [226g] package)

any flat bottomed plastic container approximately 6" × 6" (15cm × 15cm) and 1" (3cm) deep

knife

craft stick

small amount of flour

ballpoint pen

2 2-cup (470mL) microwave-safe glass measuring cups

approximately 1 lb. (.5kg) white soap base (see step 5 to determine exact amount)

brown oxide colorant

red and yellow nonbleeding liquid colorants

½ tsp. (2.5mL) strawberry fragrance oil

rubbing alcohol in spray bottle

cutting board

butter knife (optional)

heart-shaped cookie cutter

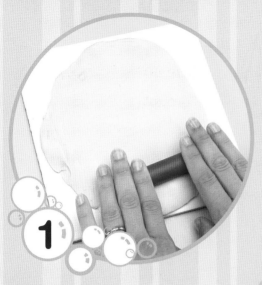

Roll out Elasticlay

On the ceramic tile or the bottom of the glass pie plate, use the small rolling pin to roll out the Elasticlay to ¼" (6mm) thickness. If the Elasticlay gets sticky, put it in the freezer for 3 minutes to stiffen it.

Cut Elasticlay

Press the bottom of the plastic container into the clay; it will leave an indent. Using the knife, cut the Elasticlay slightly smaller than the impression of the bottom of the plastic container.

Trimming the clay now helps to conserve the clay for another design. If you don't want to trim the clay at this time, it can be trimmed after it has been baked and cooled by using a pair of scissors.

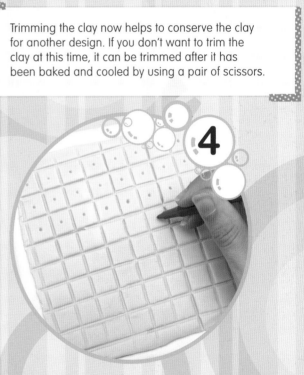

Create design

Dip the edge of the craft stick in the flour and shake off the excess. Using the edge of the craft stick, stamp rows and columns into the clay, about ½" (1cm) apart, creating a grid pattern. Move the craft stick as needed to make a complete line across the clay.

Finish design

Using the point of the ballpoint pen, make dots in the center of each square of the grid pattern.

Measure soap

Bake the clay according to the package directions. Allow it to cool. To determine how much soap to melt, pour water into the plastic container to ¾" (2cm) deep. Empty the water into the microwave-safe glass measuring cup and note the measurement. (In this case, I measured 14 oz. [396mL].)

5

Make sure the water doesn't go to the top if the cookie cutter. If it does, you'll have a hard time cutting the soap after it's unmolded.

6

Add brown layer

In one of the measuring cups, melt half of the white soap base you need to fill the mold (for me, 7 oz. [198g]). Add the brown oxide colorant (see Technique, page 13) to make a light brown color, then add a few drops of yellow to make a realistic waffle color (see Technique, page 11). Place the texture sheet grid side up into the container. Pour half of the melted brown soap on top of the Elasticlay sheet.

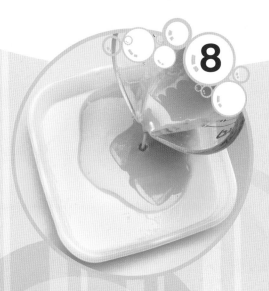

Add pink layer

Allow the soap layer to harden. In the other measuring cup, melt the remaining white soap base. Add enough red colorant to get a nice pink color. Add the fragrance oil (see Technique, page 15). Spray the brown soap in the pan with rubbing alcohol. Pour all of the pink soap into the pan.

Add final brown layer

Let the soap harden. Spray the soap in the pan with rubbing alcohol. Pour the remaining brown soap into the pan (you may need to reheat the brown soap if it has started to solidify in the cup).

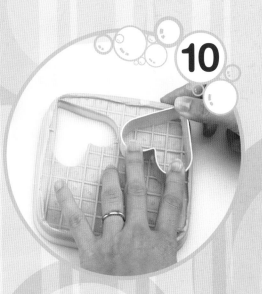

Remove clay

Allow the soap to harden. Unmold the soap by flipping the mold over and pushing on the bottom of the mold. Place the soap sheet on the cutting board. Peel the texture sheet off the soap. You may need to use a butter knife to pry an edge out of the soap before peeling the Elasticlay off completely.

Cut soaps

Using the heart-shaped cookie cutter, cut the soap sheet into bars.

Glycerin soap and chocolate are similar in that they are melted and become solid as they cool. As a result, many fun tools used for chocolate making can be used for soaps. This project shows how a high-end chocolate-making embellishment—cocoa transfer sheets—can add vivid graphic designs on the soap's surface. The number of transfer sheet designs available is amazing. Best of all, it's really easy and fun! This project makes one tray of soap, which you can cut into any number of bars.

CRAZY CIRCLES SOAPS

NOTE

It's important to note that food coloring is used to create the designs on the transfer sheets, so some of the colors will eventually bleed. As long as you use the soaps within one week it's not that noticeable. I have found that the gold and white designs do not bleed, though.

MATERIALS

scissors

"Crop Circles" chocolate transfer sheet

8" or 9" (20cm or 23cm) square silicone brownie pan, with shiny inner surface

cellophane tape

4-cup (940mL) microwave-safe glass measuring cup

1½ lb. (.75kg) white soap base

½ tsp. (2.5mL) raspberry fragrance oil (or any scent you like)

cutting board

circle cookie cutter

Prepare transfer sheet

Using the scissors, trim the transfer sheet to the size of the silicone pan. Place the transfer sheet rough side up in the pan. Using your hands, gently press out any air bubbles.

Secure transfer sheet

Using the cellophane tape, secure the corners of the transfer sheet to the pan. Try to cover as little of the design as possible.

Pour soap

In the microwave-safe glass measuring cup, melt all of the white soap base. Add the fragrance oil (see Technique, page 15). Allow the melted soap to cool to between 110-120°F (43-49°C). Pour the soap very slowly and gently over the transfer sheet.

Remove transfer sheet

Allow the soap to harden. Unmold the soap by flipping the mold over and peeling the mold away. Lay the soap sheet design side up on the cutting board. Find a corner of the transfer sheet and gently pull it off of the soap.

Cut soaps

Using the circle cookie cutter, cut the soap sheet into individual soaps.

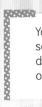

You want to pour this soap very cool so you don't melt the design on the transfer sheet.

I find an endless supply of design ideas from candy, especially the really fancy, expensive ones! These little gems use the same techniques chocolate makers use, but don't look so similar that you have to worry about people eating them. Set each soap in a truffle paper and group them into little acetate boxes for a very impressive favor at your next party! This project makes eight mixed mini soaps.

SOAP CANDIES

MATERIALS

ruler

4-cavity basic rectangular soap mold

scissors

"Candy Stripe" chocolate transfer sheet

cellophane tape

1½ lb. (.75kg) white soap base

2 2-cup (470mL) microwave-safe glass measuring cups

red nonbleeding liquid colorant

½ tsp. (2.5mL) strawberry fragrance oil

rubbing alcohol in spray bottle

cutting board

assorted mini fondant cutters

tip

For larger quantities, you can use the silicone brownie pans or any other larger plastic containers instead of the smaller rectangle molds.

NOTE

It's important to note that food coloring is used to create the designs on the transfer sheets, so some of the colors will eventually bleed. As long as you use the soaps within 1 week it's not that noticeable. I have found, however, that the gold and white transfer sheet designs do not bleed.

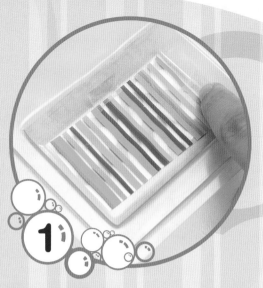

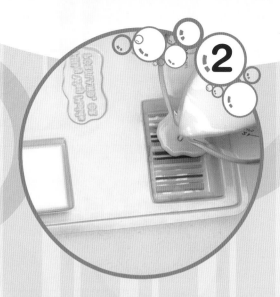

Prepare transfer sheet

Using the ruler, measure the surface of the rectangular mold. Using the scissors, cut the transfer sheet to fit 2 of the cavities. Place the transfer sheet pieces rough side up into the 2 of the molds. Using the cellophane tape, secure the sides of the transfer sheets to the sides of the mold. Try to cover as little of the design as possible.

Pour first layers

Divide the white soap base in half. Melt each half in separate microwave-safe glass measuring cups. In one cup, stir in a few drops of red colorant to achieve a bright pink color (see Technique, page 11). Add the fragrance oil (see Technique, page 15). Do not color or fragrance the other portion. Allow both cups of soap to cool to 110-120°F (43-46°C). Gently pour the white soap into 1 empty cavity, and then 1 cavity with a transfer sheet, filling each only ⅓ full.

Pour pink layer

Gently pour the pink soap into the remaining 2 empty cavities, filling only ⅓ full.

Pour alternating layer

Let the soap in the mold cool and harden. Using a spray bottle filled with rubbing alcohol, spray the soap in the molds. Pour a layer of the opposite color into each cavity. Reheat the melted soap if needed.

Finish layers
Let the second layers harden. Repeat step 4, alternating the colors, to top off each cavity.

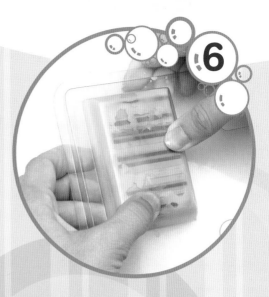

Unmold soaps
Let the soaps harden. Place the mold into the freezer for 5 minutes. Remove the mold from the freezer. Unmold the soaps by flipping the molds over and gently pushing on them to pop the soaps out onto the cutting board.

Remove transfer sheet
Find a corner of the transfer sheet and peel the sheet off of the soap.

Cut soaps
Using the mini fondant cutters, cut shapes out of each bar.

If you're making favors, combine the shapes so each box gets a mixed assortment.

Sometimes it seems like a shame to create a surface texture on a soap that will get washed off quickly. This technique uses pottery tools to put your design inside the bar so it will last much longer! Since you create the carved design, you can use any simple or fancy font you like.

MONOGRAM BARS

MATERIALS

printed letters or paper and marker

scissors

2-cup (470mL) microwave-safe glass measuring cup

4 oz. (113g) clear soap base

purple nonbleeding liquid colorant

4-cavity soap mold with flat faces

ballpoint pen

basic pottery tool kit with loop tool, ribbon tool and pointed wooden tool

¼ tsp. (1.25mL) lavender fragrance oil or any scent you like

1 lb. (.5kg) white soap base

rubbing alcohol in spray bottle

Prepare monogram

Print out or draw a letter that will fit the face of the soap mold. Make sure it's a dark color that you can see through the paper from the back. Using the scissors, cut out the desired letters, leaving a border but making them small enough to fit into the mold.

Prepare soaps

In the microwave-safe glass measuring cup, melt 4 oz. (113g) of the clear soap base. Add purple colorant until you get a sheer color (see Technique, page 11). Pour the soap into each mold to ¼" (6mm) thickness. Allow it to cool to room temperature. Place the letter face down on top of the hardened soap in the mold. Using the ballpoint pen, trace around the letter, creating an indentation in the soap.

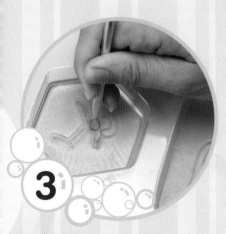

Carve letters

Use the pottery tools, carve out the letter design to about ⅛" (3mm) depth.

Pour layer

In the microwave-safe glass measuring cup, melt the white soap base. Add the fragrance oil (see Technique, page 15). Allow the melted soap to cool to 120°F (49°C). Spray the soap in the molds with rubbing alcohol. Pour the white soap in to fill each cavity.

Unmold soaps

Spray the white soap with rubbing alcohol to pop any surface bubbles. Allow the soaps to harden. Unmold the soap by flipping the mold over and pushing gently on the cavity to pop the soaps out.

The loop tool is great for curvy designs and the ribbon tool works well for crisp, linear designs. Use the pointed tool for thinner lines.

If you're having trouble unmolding the soaps, put the mold in the freezer for a few minutes and try again.

This is the advanced version of the *Monogram Bars*. This time you are carving out a design that will have contrasting colors that really stand out when the soaps are complete. The wood grain design is great because it's easy to freehand and appeals to men—some of the hardest people to think of gifts for. Everyone loves the maple syrup fragrance, too!

MAPLE BARS

 MATERIALS

2-cup (470mL) microwave-safe glass measuring cup

14 oz. (113g) ultra clear soap base

8" or 9" (20cm or 23cm) square silicone brownie pan with shiny inner surface

pointed wooden tool from a basic pottery tool kit

fork

brown oxide colorant

rubbing alcohol in spray bottle

metal spatula or scraper

12 oz. (340g) white soap base

½ tsp. (2.5mL) maple syrup fragrance oil

cutting board

Prepare design

In the microwave-safe glass measuring cup, melt 8 oz. (226g) of ultra clear soap base. Pour it into the silicone pan. Let the soap set to room temperature. Using the pointed wooden tool, draw small vertical ovals randomly into the clear soap (these are the wood knots). Use the fork to draw vertical lines that curve around the knots.

This is a very forgiving soap design. It's OK if there are bits of soap left on top of the carving, they will melt away when you add the next layer. And if you think you messed up the wood-grain look, think again. The little variations you make only mimic those found in nature.

Chisel design

Using the pointed wooden tool, deepen all of the grooves to ⅛"–¼" (3mm–6mm) depth.

Pour layer

Melt 6 oz. (170g) of the ultra clear soap base. Add the brown oxide (see Techniques, page 13) to make a rich brown color. Allow the soap to cool to 120°F (49°C). Spray the soap in the mold with rubbing alcohol. Pour the brown soap into the pan, just until the surface of the carved soap is covered.

Scrape off layer

Let the soap set for 2 minutes. Using the metal spatula, scrape the brown soap off of the surface, leaving the carved lines filled with the brown soap. Be sure to make smooth, level passes with the spatula, working with the grain, over the entire surface. Turn the pan as necessary to scrape the sides. Remove the soap from the spatula as needed. Save the scrapings for step 5.

Pour final layer

In the microwave-safe glass measuring cup, melt all of the white soap base. Mix in some of the brown soap scraps from step 4 to make a light brown color. Add the fragrance oil (see Technique, page 15). Let the melted soap cool to 120°F (49°C). Spray soap in the pan with rubbing alcohol. Pour the light brown soap into the pan.

Unmold and cut soap

Spray the soap with rubbing alcohol to pop any surface bubbles. Let the soap harden. Unmold the soap by flipping the mold over and peeling it away. Place the soap sheet wood grain side up on the cutting board. Cut the soap into bars by following the Technique on page 19.

index

IF FUN AND FUNKY IS YOUR THING, CHECK OUT THESE BOOKS!

STRAY SOCK SEWING
By Daniel

Stray Sock Sewing is a lovable Asian-flavored craft book that blends how-to projects with whimsical narrative. You'll learn how to make odd and endearing one-of-a-kind creatures from a variety of sock styles.

ISBN 13: 978-1-60061-199-5
ISBN 10: 1-60061-199-0
paperback, 144 pages, Z2799

KAWAII NOT
By Meghan Murphy

This collection features 100 original comics from the hysterical Kawaii Not comic strip, which depicts cute versions of everyday objects doing and saying some crazy stuff. The book includes stickers—nothing is more kawaii than stickers (except maybe kittens or kittens on stickers). The book will also include a "How Kawaii Are You?" quiz and the Kawaii Horoscope.

ISBN 13: 978-1-60061-076-9
ISBN 10: 1-60061-076-5
paperback, 208 pages, Z1845

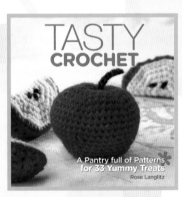

TASTY CROCHET
By Rose Langlitz

In this adorable Amigurumi-style book, you will receive patterns and helpful instruction for creating 33 projects (plus several variations for added inspiration), divided into chapters according to meal selection. Crochet a yummy set of play food, like cute, crocheted toaster pastry or bacon and eggs, that is sure to make you giggle as each piece works up quickly.

ISBN 13: 978-1-60061-312-8
ISBN 10: 1-60061-312-8
paperback, 144 pages, Z2914

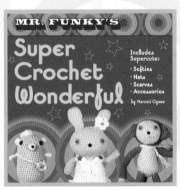

MR. FUNKY'S SUPER CROCHET WONDERFUL
By Narumi Ogawa

Mr. Funky's Super Crochet Wonderful is filled with 25 supercute crochet patterns for adorable Japanese-style stuffed animals and accessories. You'll find candy-color elephants, panda bears, kitty cats, hamsters and even a snake, plus fashionable hats, armwarmers and purses for girls of all ages. Each pattern features written out instructions as well as traditional amigurumi, or Japanese crochet diagrams.

ISBN 13: 978-1-58180-966-4
ISBN 10: 1-58180-966-2
paperback, 112 pages, Z0697

These and other North Light titles are available at your favorite local craft retailer, bookstore or online supplier, or visit our Web site at www.mycraftivity.com.

128